ADHD COOKBOOK

MAIN COURSE – 80+ Effective recipes designed to improve focus, self control and execution skills (Autism & ADD friendly recipes)

TABLE OF CONTENTS

BREAKFAST 7
EGGS RANCHERO 7
BREAKFAST BURRITO 8
BREAKFAST MUFFINS 9
BREAKFAST PORRIDGE 10
CREPES 12
BLUEBERRY FRENCH TOAST 13
FRITTATA 14
MAPLE BREAD 16
SIMPLE PANCAKES 17
PUMPKIN PANCAKES 18
SEAFOOD OMELET 19
MORNING COOKIES 20
BAKED OATMEAL 21
BAKED OMELET 23
EGG-IN-A-HOLE 24
MINI FRITTATAS 25
MINI QUICHES 26
CHIA PUDDING 28
PEANUT BUTTER OATMEAL 29
BREAKFATS BURRITO 30
DINNER 59
CHICKEN WITH CAULIFLOWER AND OLIVES 59
ROSEMARY LEMON CHICKEN 60
SALMON BURGERS 61

ARGULA CUCUMBER SALAD	62
TURKEY TACOS	63
AVOCADO BACON AND EGGS	65
EGGS BAKED IN MUSHROOMS	66
TURMERIC CAULIFLOWER	67
QUINOA SALAD	68
MEXICAN PIZZA	69
CHICKEN PIZZA	70
TURKEY MEATLOAF	71
FRITTATA	72
SLOPPY JOE SLIDERS	74
SPINACH BALLS	75
ZUCCHINI PIZZA	76
CARROT AND BROCCOLI NUGGETS	77
PIZZA PASTA	79
CHICKEN VEGGIE BAKE	80
CHICKEN WITH ROASTED PEPPERS	81
LUNCH	**32**
GRILLED CHICKEN WITH SPINACH AND MOZZARELLA	32
CABBAGE SKILLET	33
BROCCOLI CHEESE CHICKEN	35
FISH STICKS	37
STUFFED CABBAGE	38
ASPARAGUS SOUP	40
CARROT SOUP	41
MEXICAN CHICKEN	42

GRILLED SALMON 43

MEXICAN QUINOA 44

TACO SKILLET 45

QUINOA WITH SWEET POTATOES AND CINNAMON 46

CHINESE CHICKEN BOWL 48

BEEF BOURGUIGNON 49

MINESTRONE SOUP 50

CIOPPINO 51

BUTTERNUT STEW 53

KALE SALAD WITH CHICKEN 54

CHICKEN LENTIL SOUP 55

SHRIMP CHOWDER 57

DESSERT 83

PUMPKIN BISCUITS 83

SESAME ALMOND BARS 84

STRAWBERRY CUPCAKES 85

PIZZA SNACKS 86

ROASTED CRISPS 88

POPSICLES 89

BUTTER CUPS 90

BEET & CAULIFLOWER TORTILLAS 91

BLUEBERRY MUFFINS 92

CHOCOLATE THINS 94

DRINKS 95

ROOT BEER FLOAT 95

CHERRY SMOOTHIE 96

PUMPKIN CAPPUCCINO 97

MORNING SMOOTHIE 98

MANGO PASSION SMOOTHIE 99

HEARTBEET SMOOTHIE 100

ENERGY SMOOTHIE 101

CHOCOLATE SMOOTHIE 102

START SMOOTHIE 103

ANTIOXIDANT SMOOTHIE 104

Copyright 2018 by Noah Jerris - All rights reserved.

This document is geared towards providing exact and reliable information in regards to the topic and issue covered. The publication is sold with the idea that the publisher is not required to render accounting, officially permitted, or otherwise, qualified services. If advice is necessary, legal or professional, a practiced individual in the profession should be ordered.

- From a Declaration of Principles which was accepted and approved equally by a Committee of the American Bar Association and a Committee of Publishers and Associations.

In no way is it legal to reproduce, duplicate, or transmit any part of this document in either electronic means or in printed format. Recording of this publication is strictly prohibited and any storage of this document is not allowed unless with written permission from the publisher. All rights reserved.

The information provided herein is stated to be truthful and consistent, in that any liability, in terms of inattention or otherwise, by any usage or abuse of any policies, processes, or directions contained within is the solitary and utter responsibility of the recipient reader. Under no circumstances will any legal responsibility or blame be held against the publisher for any reparation, damages, or monetary loss due to the information herein, either directly or indirectly.

Respective authors own all copyrights not held by the publisher.

The information herein is offered for informational purposes solely, and is universal as so. The presentation of the information is without contract or any type of guarantee assurance.

The trademarks that are used are without any consent, and the publication of the trademark is without permission or backing by the trademark owner. All trademarks and brands within this book are for clarifying purposes only and are the owned by the owners themselves, not affiliated with this document.

Introduction

ADHD recipes to improve focus but also for family enjoyment. You will love them for sure for how easy it is to prepare them.

BREAKFAST

EGGS RANCHERO

Serves: 2

Prep Time: 5 Minutes

Cook Time: 10 Minutes

Total Time: 15 Minutes

INGREDIENTS

- 1 tsp pepper
- 2 eggs
- 1 cup kidney beans
- 1 garlic clove
- 2 cups spinach
- 3 tbs salsa
- ½ tsp cumin
- 1 tsp paprika
- 1 tsp salt
- 2 tsp oil
- 2 shallots

DIRECTIONS

1. Heat 1 tsp oil.
2. Saute the garlic and shallots for 3 minutes.

3. Add the beans, cumin, paprika and season with pepper.
4. Cook the beans for 5 minutes.
5. Set aside and keep warm.
6. Beat the eggs in a bowl.
7. Heat the rest of the oil in a skillet and cook the eggs, seasoning with salt and pepper.
8. Place the spinach on a plate, then top with the eggs and salsa.

BREAKFAST BURRITO

Serves: 2

Prep Time: 5 Minutes

Cook Time: 5 Minutes

Total Time: **10** Minutes

INGREDIENTS

- ½ onion
- 4 lettuce leaves
- 2 tsp salsa
- 2 eggs
- 4 egg whites
- ½ cup mushrooms
- ½ avocado

- 1 garlic clove
- ½ cup red pepper
- ½ cup broccoli florets
- 2 tsp oil

DIRECTIONS

1. Whisk the eggs and egg whites.
2. Heat the oil in a skillet.
3. Saute the onion and garlic for 1 minute.
4. Add the mushrooms, broccoli and bell pepper and cook for 33-4 minutes.
5. Add the eggs and stir until cooked.

BREAKFAST MUFFINS

Serves: 8

Prep Time: 10 Minutes

Cook Time: 25 Minutes

Total Time: 35 Minutes

INGREDIENTS

- 1 cup scallions
- ½ tsp black pepper

- 5 bacon pieces
- 1 cooked potato
- 10 eggs
- 1 tsp salt
- ½ tsp garlic powder
- ¼ cup water

DIRECTIONS

1. Preheat the oven to 350F.
2. Grease the muffin pan.
3. Beat the eggs in a bowl.
4. Stir in the potato, scallions, salt, pepper and garlic powder.
5. Mix in the bacon.
6. Spoon into the muffin cups until half full.
7. Bake for 25 minutes.
8. Cool, then serve.

BREAKFAST PORRIDGE

Serves: 4

Prep Time: 5 Minutes

Cook Time: 5 Minutes

Total Time: *10* Minutes

INGREDIENTS

- ¼ tsp nutmeg
- ½ cup butter
- 1 tsp vanilla
- 1 ½ tbs pumpkin pie spice
- 2 cups coconut milk
- 3 tbs cocoa powder
- 2 tbs maple syrup
- 2 ½ tbs raisins
- 2 bananas
- 1 cup water
- 1 cup flour
- ½ cup flax meal
- 1 ½ tbs coconut
- 2 tbs coconut chips
- 2 scoops protein powder
- 2 tsp cinnamon
- ¼ tsp ground cloves

DIRECTIONS

1. Mix all of the ingredients except for the protein powder in a saucepan.
2. Heat to a simmer until thick.
3. Stir in the protein powder during the last 2 minutes.
4. Add 1 cup coconut milk to create the desired consistency.
5. Sprinkle with any toppings and serve.

CREPES

Serves: **4**

Prep Time: **10** Minutes

Cook Time: **5** Minutes

Total Time: **15** Minutes

INGREDIENTS

- 2 tsp vanilla
- 2 cups flour
- 3 tbs flaxseed meal
- 1 cup strawberries
- 3 tbs carob chips
- 5 egg whites
- 1 cup almond milk
- 1 cup coconut milk
- 3 tsp cinnamon
- 1 cup blueberries
- 3 tbs erythritol
- 2 tsp baking powder

DIRECTIONS

1. Puree the strawberries for the topping, then set aside.
2. Mix the dry ingredients in a bowl.

3. Add the almond milk, egg whites and vanilla.
4. Beat until smooth.
5. Use ¼ cup of batter for 1 pancake.
6. Cook the pancake for 1 minute on one side and 30 seconds on the other.
7. Put blueberries on the crepe, then roll it.
8. Put the rolled crepes back in the pan for 30 seconds per side.
9. Place them on a plate and garnish with the strawberry topping.

BLUEBERRY FRENCH TOAST

Serves: 2
Prep Time: *10* Minutes
Cook Time: *30* Minutes
Total Time: *40* Minutes

INGREDIENTS

- 3 tbs maple syrup
- ¼ tsp cinnamon
- 2 slices bread
- 2 eggs
- 2 egg whites

- ½ cup coconut oil

DIRECTIONS

1. Whip the eggs, egg whites and cinnamon in a bowl.
2. Soak the bread in the mixture for at least 20 seconds.
3. Heat the oil in a pan.
4. Add the bread when the oil is hot enough.
5. Cook until brown, then flip over.
6. Place the bread on a plate and top with blueberries and maple syrup.
7. Serve hot.

FRITTATA

Serves: **6**

Prep Time: **10** Minutes

Cook Time: **10** Minutes

Total Time: **20** Minutes

INGREDIENTS

- 8 ounces chicken breast
- 2 tsp salt
- 1 tsp black pepper

- 1 red pepper
- 2 garlic cloves
- 3 tomatoes
- 1 cup spinach
- 2 tsp oil
- 8 eggs
- 1 avocado
- 1 tbs thyme
- 1 ½ tbs marjoram
- 2 scallions

DIRECTIONS

1. Preheat the oven to broil.
2. Heat the oil in a skillet.
3. Cook the red peppers and scallions for 3 minutes.
4. Add the chicken, thyme, garlic, tomatoes, marjoram, salt and pepper and cook for another minute.
5. Add the spinach and cook 1 more minute.
6. Add the eggs to the skillet and cook until the eggs begin to set.
7. Put the skillet in the oven for 5 minutes.
8. Serve sliced and topped with avocado slices.

MAPLE BREAD

Serves: **4**

Prep Time: **10** Minutes

Cook Time: **30** Minutes

Total Time: **40** Minutes

INGREDIENTS

- 1 tsp baking soda
- 1 ½ tbs vanilla
- 1 lemon zest
- 1 tsp salt
- 6 eggs
- 2 cups flour
- ½ cup maple syrup
- 1 ½ tsp vinegar
- ½ cup flax meal
- ½ cup oil

DIRECTIONS

1. Preheat the oven to 350F.
2. Mix the dry ingredients in a bowl.
3. In another bowl, mix the eggs, vinegar and maple syrup, then add vanilla, oil and lemon zest.
4. Blend well.

5. Add the blended ingredients in the dry ingredients bowl.
6. Mix well.
7. Pour the mixture into mini-loaf pans.
8. Bake in the oven for 30 minutes.
9. Allow to cool, then serve.

SIMPLE PANCAKES

Serves: 2

Prep Time: 5 Minutes

Cook Time: 5 Minutes

Total Time: 10 Minutes

INGREDIENTS

- 2 tbs flax meal
- 2 tsp maple syrup
- 2 tsp oil
- 1 ½ banana
- 1 cup strawberries
- 4 eggs
- 1 ½ tsp arrowroot
- 1 tsp almond butter

DIRECTIONS

1. Blend the strawberries, then set aside.
2. Place all ingredients in a bowl and blend until smooth.
3. Heat the oil in a pan.
4. Pour ¼ cup of the batter in the pan.
5. Cook 35 seconds on each side.
6. Serve topped with the strawberry sauce.

PUMPKIN PANCAKES

Serves: 2

Prep Time: 5 Minutes

Cook Time: 5 Minutes

Total Time: 10 Minutes

INGREDIENTS

- 1 tbs almond butter
- 2 tsp oil
- 2 tbs flax meal
- 3 eggs
- 1 cup pumpkin
- 2 tsp maple syrup
- 2 tsp pumpkin pie spice
- 1 ½ tsp arrowroot

DIRECTIONS

1. Mix the pumpkin pie spice, flax meal and arrowroot in a bowl.
2. Blend the eggs, almond butter, pumpkin and the dry ingredients until well combined.
3. Warm some oil in a skillet.
4. Add the batter to the skillet and cook for 35 seconds per side.
5. Serve topped with maple syrup.

SEAFOOD OMELET

Serves: 2

Prep Time: 10 Minutes

Cook Time: 30 Minutes

Total Time: 40 Minutes

INGREDIENTS

- 2 egg whites
- 2 tsp butter
- 1 chive
- 5 shrimp
- 2 tsp oil
- 1 tsp ginger

- 5 green onions
- ½ cup bean sprouts
- 1 tsp pepper
- 5 scallops
- 2 eggs

DIRECTIONS

1. Heat the oil in a skillet.
2. Saute the onions and ginger for 1 minute.
3. Add the scallops and shrimp and cook for another minute, then set aside.
4. Mix the eggs and egg whites with the pepper in a bowl.
5. Heat a butter coated skillet.
6. Pour the eggs into the skillet and cook for 1-2 minutes, then flip over and cook for 1 more minute.
7. Top with the cooked seafood, bean sprouts and chives and serve.

MORNING COOKIES

Serves: **20**
Prep Time: **5** Minutes
Cook Time: **25** Minutes
Total Time: **30** Minutes

INGREDIENTS

- ½ cup chia seeds
- ½ flax seed meal
- 1 cup honey
- 1 cup butter
- 6 eggs
- ½ cup raisins
- 5 ½ cups flour

DIRECTIONS

1. Mix the oil with the eggs and the honey.
2. Add the flour and mix well.
3. Add the chia seeds, raisins and the flax seed meal.
4. Spoon the batter onto a lined cookie sheet.
5. Bake at 350F for 25 minutes.

BAKED OATMEAL

Serves: *4*
Prep Time: *10* Minutes
Cook Time: *40* Minutes

Total Time: **50** Minutes

INGREDIENTS

- 1 can pumpkin
- 1 ½ tsp baking soda
- 8 eggs
- 1 tsp salt
- 1 cup raisins
- 7 cups oats
- 2 cups yogurt
- 1 cup milk
- 1 cup honey
- ½ cup chia seeds
- 2 cups water
- ½ cup butter
- ½ cup flax seed meal

DIRECTIONS

1. Place the oats in a pan.
2. Mix in the yogurt and the water.
3. Let soak for a day.
4. Mix in the butter, milk, eggs, raisins, honey, salt, chia seeds, baking soda, flax seed meal, and the pumpkin.
5. Bake at 350F for 40 minutes.
6. Allow to cool, then serve.

BAKED OMELET

Serves: 4

Prep Time: 10 Minutes

Cook Time: 50 Minutes

Total Time: 60 Minutes

INGREDIENTS

- ½ cup green onion
- 1 cup ham
- 8 eggs
- 1 lb bread
- 2 lb cheese
- 2 cups milk
- 2 tsp salt

DIRECTIONS

1. Preheat the oven to 350F.
2. Grease a baking dish.
3. Cut the bread into cubes and place them on the bottom of the baking dish.
4. Sprinkle half of the ham and cheese, then repeat.
5. Beat the eggs, milk, salt and green onions in a bowl.
6. Pour the mixture into the pan.
7. Place on top of a baking sheet with a rim.

8. Pour water into the baking sheet and bake for 50 minutes.

EGG-IN-A-HOLE

Serves: **4**

Prep Time: **5** Minutes

Cook Time: **5** Minutes

Total Time: **10** Minutes

INGREDIENTS

- 1 tbs oil
- 2 tsp salt
- 1 tsp pepper
- 1 bell pepper
- 4 eggs
- ½ cup cheese

DIRECTIONS

1. Heat the oil in a skillet.
2. Cut the pepper into rings and remove the seeds and centers.
3. Place them into the skillet and saute for a minute.
4. Crack the eggs into each ring.

5. Sprinkle salt and pepper.
6. Cook for 3 minutes, then flip over.
7. Top with cheese, and cook for another minute.
8. Serve immediately.

MINI FRITTATAS

Serves: 6

Prep Time: 20 Minutes

Cook Time: 30 Minutes

Total Time: 50 Minutes

INGREDIENTS

- 2 cups tomatoes
- 1 cup onion
- ¼ tsp salt
- 4 2-ounces links chicken sausage
- 8 eggs
- 2 tsp oil
- 2 potatoes
- 1 cup yogurt
- 2 cloves garlic

DIRECTIONS

1. Preheat the oven to 400F.
2. Heat the oil in a skillet.
3. Add the onions, potatoes and salt.
4. Saute for 10 minutes.
5. Add the sausage, garlic and tomatoes and saute for another 3 minutes.
6. Divide the mixture among muffin tins.
7. Allow to cool.
8. Whisk the eggs and yogurt in a bowl.
9. Stir in the basil, pepper, and cheese.
10. Divide among the muffin cups.
11. Bake for 20 minutes.
12. Allow to cool, then serve.

MINI QUICHES

Serves: **8**

Prep Time: **10** Minutes

Cook Time: **20** Minutes

Total Time: **30** Minutes

INGREDIENTS

- ½ tsp black pepper

- 1 cup heavy cream
- 2 tsp salt
- 1 cup cheese
- 1 cup milk
- ½ head broccoli
- 6 eggs
- 6 egg yolks

DIRECTIONS

1. Preheat the oven to 375F.
2. Line 24-cup muffin pans with paper liners.
3. Bring a saucepan of water to a boil.
4. Add the broccoli and blanch for 30 seconds.
5. Transfer immediately to a bowl of ice water.
6. Allow to cool, then drain and chop.
7. Whisk the eggs, egg yolks, salt, milk, cream and pepper in a bowl.
8. Put some small pieces of broccoli and some cheese in the muffin cups, then pour the egg mixture over.
9. Top with a pinch of cheese.
10. Bake for 15 minutes.
11. Allow to cool, then serve.

CHIA PUDDING

Serves: 2

Prep Time: 5 Minutes

Cook Time: 0 Minutes

Total Time: 5 Minutes

INGREDIENTS

- 1 ½ tsp cinnamon
- ½ cup butter
- 1 cup milk
- 2 tsp vanilla
- 3 tbs chia seeds
- 1 banana

DIRECTIONS

1. Blend all of the ingredients except for the chia seeds.
2. Transfer to a jar, then stir in the chia seeds.
3. Refrigerate overnight.
4. Top with the sliced banana.

PEANUT BUTTER OATMEAL

Serves: **4**

Prep Time: **10** Minutes

Cook Time: **7** Hours

Total Time: **7h 10** Minutes

INGREDIENTS

- 1 tbs chia seeds
- 1 ½ tsp cinnamon
- 2 tsp vanilla
- 3 cups milk
- ½ cup peanut butter
- 2 bananas
- 1 cup oats

DIRECTIONS

1. Mix all of the ingredients in a bowl.
2. Place the bowl in the slow cooker, then fill the slow cooker with 1 cup water.
3. Cook for 7 hours.
4. Remove the bowl, then serve.

BREAKFATS BURRITO

Serves: **4**

Prep Time: **10** Minutes

Cook Time: **25** Minutes

Total Time: **35** Minutes

INGREDIENTS

- 8 tortillas
- 2 cups cheese
- 1 tsp salt
- 3 cups hash browns
- 10 slices bacon
- 12 eggs
- ½ cup milk
- 1 cup ham
- ½ tsp black pepper
- ½ tsp paprika

DIRECTIONS

1. Cook the hash browns.
2. Cook the bacon until crispy, then set aside.
3. Whisk the eggs, milk, salt, pepper, and paprika.
4. Heat a drizzle of oil in a skillet.

5. Pour the egg mixture into the skillet and cook for 5 minutes.
6. Top the tortillas with bacon, eggs, potatoes, ham and cheese, then roll them up.

LUNCH

GRILLED CHICKEN WITH SPINACH AND MOZZARELLA

Serves: **4**

Prep Time: **10** Minutes

Cook Time: **15** Minutes

Total Time: **25** Minutes

INGREDIENTS

- 2 tsp salt
- 1 tsp black pepper
- 1 ½ tsp oil
- 3 cloves garlic
- 4 ounces mozzarella
- 1 cup red pepper
- 2 tsp oil
- 3 chicken breasts
- 12 ounces spinach

DIRECTIONS

1. Preheat the oven to 400F.
2. Season the chicken with salt and pepper.
3. Spray a pan with oil.
4. Cook the chicken for 3 minutes on each side.

5. Heat a skillet.
6. Saute the garlic and the onion for 35 seconds, then add the spinach, salt and pepper and cook for 3 minutes.
7. Place the chicken on a baking sheet, then top with the spinach.
8. Sprinkle the mozzarella over, add the roasted peppers on top and bake for 3 minutes.

CABBAGE SKILLET

Serves: 4
Prep Time: 20 Minutes
Cook Time: 35 Minutes
Total Time: 55 Minutes

INGREDIENTS

- 2 tsp oil
- 1 onion
- 1 carrot
- 2 tbs tomato paste
- 1 ½ tsp salt
- 1 tsp black pepper
- 8 potatoes
- ½ cabbage head

- 5 sausages

DIRECTIONS

1. Cut the peeled potatoes.
2. Fry the potatoes in the oil, in a kettle.
3. Chop the onion and grate the carrot.
4. After 5 minutes, add the onion and carrot to the kettle and cook for another 5 minutes.
5. Chop the cabbage.
6. Add the cabbage to the vegetables, cover it and stew for 8 minutes.
7. Open the lid and allow to fry for 10 minutes.
8. Stir in from time to time.
9. Cut the sausages and add to vegetables.
10. Cook covered for another 5 minutes.
11. Pour 2 tbs of tomato paste and allow to fry for 2 minutes.
12. Pour 1 cup water, season with salt and pepper, mix and cook covered for another 5 minutes.
13. Put away from the heat and allow to infuse for another 10 minutes.

BROCCOLI CHEESE CHICKEN

Serves: **6**

Prep Time: **10** Minutes

Cook Time: **50** Minutes

Total Time: **60** Minutes

INGREDIENTS

- 1 tsp black pepper
- 3 cups broccoli florets
- ½ cup water
- 1 ½ tbs butter
- 3 ½ cup chicken broth
- 2 tbs oil
- 1 onion
- 1 cup celery
- 1 cup quinoa
- 1 ½ tsp chicken seasoning
- 3 cloves garlic
- 2 chicken breasts
- 2 cups cheese
- 1 cup bread crumbs
- 2 ½ tbs flour
- 1 cup milk
- 2 tsp salt

DIRECTIONS

1. Preheat the oven to 350F.
2. Pour 2 cups chicken broth in a saucepan and bring to a boil.
3. Cover and simmer for 20 minutes,
4. Remove from heat and set aside covered for 10 minutes.
5. Microwave the broccoli with water for 2 minutes, then set aside.
6. Heat 1 tbs of oil and 1 tbs of butter.
7. Sauté the celery and onion for 5 minutes.
8. Add the garlic and sauté for another minute.
9. Stir in the flour and cook for another 1 minute.
10. Pour 1 cup chicken broth and 1 cup milk, then stir.
11. Add the chicken seasoning, salt and pepper.
12. Turn to simmer for 5 minutes.
13. Remove from heat, then pour over the broccoli.
14. Add quinoa, chicken and half of the cheese, then stir.
15. Pour the mixture into a baking dish.
16. Sprinkle the remaining cheese and breadcrumbs on top.
17. Bake for 25 minutes.
18. Allow to cool, then serve.

FISH STICKS

Serves: **4**

Prep Time: **10** Minutes

Cook Time: **30** Minutes

Total Time: **40** Minutes

INGREDIENTS

- 2 tbs oil
- 11 tsp salt
- 1 tbs black pepper
- 1 cup flour
- 2 lb fish
- 1 tsp onion powder
- 1 tsp garlic powder
- 1 ½ cup macadamia nuts
- 3 eggs

DIRECTIONS

1. Grind the nuts until finely chopped.
2. Mix the onion powder, flour, and garlic powder.
3. Whisk the eggs in a bowl.
4. Line a cookie sheet with parchment paper, and a second cookie sheet with layers of paper towel.
5. Cut the fish into strips.

6. Place the fish sticks in the coconut flour, dusting all sides.
7. Dip the strips in the egg.
8. Roll in the ground macadamia nuts, and place on the parchment paper.
9. Heat 2 tbs of ghee in a skillet.
10. Cook the sticks evenly on all sides, until golden brown.
11. Remove the sticks and place them on the cookie sheet with paper towels.

STUFFED CABBAGE

Serves: **4**

Prep Time: **10** Minutes

Cook Time: **30** Minutes

Total Time: **40** Minutes

INGREDIENTS

- 1 ½ tsp salt
- ½ tsp black pepper
- 1 cup sauerkraut
- 1 cup rice
- 3 tbs red wine
- 1 ½ lb ground beef
- 1 lb ground pork

- 1 lb ground veal
- 2 lb green cabbage
- 2 ½ cups tomato juice
- ½ cup tomato paste
- 2 tbs white wine
- 2 tbs oil
- 1 ½ tbs sugar
- 1 tsp thyme
- ½ tsp paprika
- 4 ounces bacon
- 1 ½ cup onion
- 2 cloves garlic

DIRECTIONS

1. Cook the rice.
2. Bring a pot of salted water to a boil and sink the cabbage for 5 minutes.
3. Drain, then set aside.
4. Cook the bacon for about 5 minutes.
5. Add the onions and saute for 3 minutes.
6. Add red wine.
7. Place the three meats to the center.
8. Stir in until fully browned.
9. Add the tomato juice, tomato paste, thyme, salt, pepper, vinegar, sugar and paprika.
10. Simmer for 5 minutes.
11. Add in the cooked rice, cooked cabbage and sauerkraut.
12. Simmer for another 5 minutes.
13. Season and serve.

ASPARAGUS SOUP

Serves: **4**

Prep Time: **15** Minutes

Cook Time: **55** Minutes

Total Time: **70** Minutes

INGREDIENTS

- 1 onion
- 2 tbs coconut milk
- 2 tsp salt
- 1 lb asparagus
- 1 ½ tsp tarragon
- 1 tsp pepper
- 1 leek
- ½ cup celery
- 3 cups chicken stock
- 1 ½ tbs arrowroot
- 2 tbs oil

DIRECTIONS

1. Cut off asparagus tips.
2. Heat the oil in a soup pot.
3. Sauté the onions, celery, asparagus, leeks for 5 minutes.

4. Add the arrowroot and stir until blended for 1 minute.
5. Transfer to a blender.
6. Add 1 cup stock, then blend.
7. Add the remaining stock gradually.
8. Bring to a boil, then simmer for 35 minutes.
9. Add the coconut milk, then season with salt and pepper.
10. Add the asparagus and simmer for 10 minutes.

CARROT SOUP

Serves: *4*
Prep Time: *20* Minutes
Cook Time: *1h 35* Minutes
Total Time: *1h 55* Minutes

INGREDIENTS

- 16 ounces vegetable stock
- 2 tsp salt
- 1 tsp black pepper
- 2 onions
- 3 lbs carrots
- 1 potato
- 1 cup celery
- 4 tbs oil

DIRECTIONS

1. Cook the onions in the oil for about 1 hour.
2. Add the potato, carrots and celery for 10 minutes.
3. Add the vegetable stock and bring to a boil.
4. Cook for about 20 minutes.
5. Blend until smooth.
6. Season with salt and pepper.

MEXICAN CHICKEN

Serves: **4**

Prep Time: **10** Minutes

Cook Time: **20** Minutes

Total Time: **30** Minutes

INGREDIENTS

- 2 tsp oil
- 2 chicken breasts
- 2 bell peppers
- 2 cups broccoli florets
- 1 ½ tsp cumin
- 1 tsp cayenne pepper
- 1 tsp paprika

DIRECTIONS

1. Heat a pan.
2. Heat the oil for about 20 seconds.
3. Add diced chicken and cook for 5 minutes.
4. Add the broccoli and peppers and cook for another 10 minutes.
5. Add the spices.
6. Cook until the water is absorbed.

GRILLED SALMON

Serves: 4

Prep Time: 5 Minutes

Cook Time: 10 Minutes

Total Time: 15 Minutes

INGREDIENTS

- 2 limes juiced
- 1 tbs cilantro
- 1 ½ tsp cumin
- 1 ½ tsp paprika
- 2 lbs salmon
- 1 ½ tbs oil

- 1 tsp onion powder
- 1 tsp chili powder
- 1 avocado
- 2 tsp salt
- 1 red onion

DIRECTIONS

1. Mix the chili powder, onion powder, cumin, paprika, salt and pepper together.
2. Rub the salmon with the mix and oil.
3. Refrigerate for 30 minutes.
4. Preheat the grill.
5. Mix the avocado with lime juice, cilantro, and onion together.
6. Grill the salmon.
7. Serve topped with the avocado salsa.

MEXICAN QUINOA

Serves: 8

Prep Time: 15 Minutes

Cook Time: 4 Hours

Total Time: *4h 15* Minutes

INGREDIENTS

- 1 jalapeno
- 2 cups enchilada sauce
- 1 ½ cup chicken broth
- 1 can black beans
- 2 lb butternut squash
- 1 cup corn
- 1 cup quinoa
- 1 tsp garlic
- 1 can tomatoes

DIRECTIONS

1. Peel and deseed the butternut squash.
2. Cut into cubes, then place in the slow cooker.
3. Add the corn, quinoa, garlic, tomatoes, black beans, jalapeno, enchilada sauce and the chicken broth.
4. Give it a good stir, then cook for 4 hours.
5. Allow the liquid to absorb while on low for 30 minutes.
6. Season with salt and pepper.

TACO SKILLET

Serves: 4
Prep Time: 10 Minutes
Cook Time: 20 Minutes

Total Time: **30** Minutes

INGREDIENTS

- 3 cups kale
- 1 onion
- 2 bell peppers
- 2 zucchinis
- 1 can tomatoes
- 1 lb ground beef

DIRECTIONS

1. Cook the meat until brown.
2. Add the diced onion, peppers and zucchinis and cook until soft.
3. Add the tomatoes and stir.
4. Add the kale to a bowl and top with the taco mixture.

QUINOA WITH SWEET POTATOES AND CINNAMON

Serves: **4**

Prep Time: **20** Minutes

Cook Time: **60** Minutes

Total Time: **80** Minutes

INGREDIENTS

- 3 tbs oil
- 2 cups stock
- 2 bay leaves
- ½ cup parsley
- 2 sweet potatoes
- 2 tsp salt
- 1 cup quinoa
- 1 onion
- 2 tsp cinnamon

DIRECTIONS

1. Preheat the oven to 400F.
2. Toss the sweet potatoes with the cinnamon, 1 tbs of oil and 1 tsp salt.
3. Bake for about 20 minutes.
4. Cook the quinoa.
5. Heat the remaining oil in a saucepan.
6. Cook the onion for 5 minutes.
7. Add the quinoa.
8. Cook for another 5 minutes.
9. Add the stock and the remaining tsp of salt and the bay leaves.
10. Bring to a boil, then reduce the heat and cook for 15 minutes.
11. Remove from heat and allow to sit for 15 minutes.

CHINESE CHICKEN BOWL

Serves: **1**

Prep Time: **5** Minutes

Cook Time: **5** Minutes

Total Time: **10** Minutes

INGREDIENTS

- ½ cup green onions
- 1 cup mushrooms
- 2 tbs soy sauce
- 2 ½ cups broccoli florets
- 4 ounces chicken
- 2 cups snow peas

DIRECTIONS

1. **Combine all of the ingredients.**
2. **Serve.**

BEEF BOURGUIGNON

Serves: **6**

Prep Time: **20** Minutes

Cook Time: **5** Hours

Total Time: *5h 20* Minutes

INGREDIENTS

- 5 garlic cloves
- 1 ½ tbs herbs
- 2 tsp salt
- 3 cups red wine
- 3 lb beef roast
- 3 tbs oil
- 1 onion
- 1 cup carrots
- 7 slices bacon
- 1 tsp black pepper
- 2 tbs tomato paste

DIRECTIONS

1. Smear the oil around the bottom of a stoneware.
2. Laydown 3 pieces of bacon.
3. Add the sliced onion and garlic.

4. Put the meat on top of the onion and garlic.
5. Sprinkle the herbs over.
6. Add the tomato paste.
7. Lay the other slices of bacon on top, then add the carrots.
8. Cook covered on high for 5 hours.
9. Serve with your favourite side.

MINESTRONE SOUP

Serves: **6**

Prep Time: **10** Minutes

Cook Time: **20** Minutes

Total Time: **30** Minutes

INGREDIENTS

- 2 tsp salt
- 1 tsp black pepper
- 2 tsp thyme
- 2 bay leaves
- 1 15-ounces can tomatoes
- 3 tbs oil
- 1 onion
- 2 celery stalks
- 5 cups vegetable broth

- 2 cups kidney beans
- Noodles
- 2 cups spinach
- 1 carrot
- 1 zucchini
- 3 tbs parsley

DIRECTIONS

1. Heat 2 tbs oil.
2. Sauté the onion, celery and carrot for 5 minutes.
3. Add the zucchini, bay leaves and thyme and cook for another 2 minutes.
4. Stir in the tomatoes and vegetable broth.
5. Bring to a boil, then simmer for 10 minutes.
6. Add the spinach and parsley last.
7. Stir in and allow to sit for a minute or two.

CIOPPINO

Serves: *4*
Prep Time: *15* Minutes
Cook Time: *35* Minutes
Total Time: *50* Minutes

INGREDIENTS

- 1 lb fish
- 1 lb shrimp
- 1 lb mussels
- 1 lb bay scallops
- 2 tbs oil
- 1 tsp pepper
- 6 tbs parsley
- 2 bay leaves
- 5 garlic cloves
- 1 onion
- 1 celery stalk
- 3 cups tomatoes
- 1 15-ounces tomato sauce
- 3 cups vegetable broth
- 3 tbs shallots
- 1 ½ tsp saffron
- 2 tsp paprika
- 2 tsp salt

DIRECTIONS

1. Heat the oil.
2. Cook the celery, paprika, saffron, bay leaves, shallots and onion for 5 minutes.
3. Add the garlic and cook for another minute.
4. Add the tomatoes, tomatoe sauce and vegetable broth.
5. Bring to a boil, then simmer for 20 minutes.
6. Add the fish, scallops, shrimp and mussels.
7. Season with salt and pepper, then simmer for 5 minutes.

BUTTERNUT STEW

Serves: **8**

Prep Time: **10** Minutes

Cook Time: **35** Minutes

Total Time: **45** Minutes

INGREDIENTS

- 5 bay leaves
- 2 tbs paprika
- 14 ounces can milk
- 2 tsp salt
- 1 tsp black pepper
- 2 tbs oil
- 2 onions
- 1 tsp cinnamon
- 1 tsp nutmeg
- 2 lbs lamb
- 15 ounces can tomatoes
- 6 garlic cloves
- 3 lbs butternut squash
- 32 ounces vegetable broth
- 9 chard leaves

DIRECTIONS

1. Sauté the onions in the oil for 10 minutes.
2. Add the garlic and bay leaves and saute for 2 more minutes.
3. Add the nutmeg, paprika and cinnamon and sauté for another minute.
4. Add the lamb and sauté until the lamb is browned.
5. Add the tomatoes, broth and butternut squash.
6. Simmer covered for 15 minutes.
7. Remove from heat, and finish with coconut milk, salt and pepper.

KALE SALAD WITH CHICKEN

Serves: 6

Prep Time: 20 Minutes

Cook Time: 0 Minutes

Total Time: 20 Minutes

INGREDIENTS

- ½ tsp salt
- 1 tsp black pepper
- 2 tbs sesame seeds
- 3 tbs pecans
- 8 ounces kale

- 1 cup cilantro
- 4 cups chicken
- 1 ½ tsp honey
- 1 ½ tbs oil
- ¼ cup raisins
- 2 oranges

DIRECTIONS

1. Place the kale and cilantro in a bowl.
2. In a bowl, mix together the salt, pepper, 1 orange juice, honey, and sesame seeds.
3. Add diced orange, sesame seeds, pecans, raisins, then pour over the kale and cilantro.
4. Refrigerate for 30 minutes, serve with chicken

CHICKEN LENTIL SOUP

Serves: 4

Prep Time: 15 Minutes

Cook Time: 55 Minutes

Total Time: 70 Minutes

INGREDIENTS

- 6 cups chicken broth
- 2 tsp salt
- 1 tsp curry powder
- 1 tsp cumin
- 5 celery stalks
- 3 cups red lentils
- 2 tbs marjoram
- 2 tbs sage
- 2 carrots
- 2 tbs lemon juice
- 3 garlic cloves
- 5 cups water
- 1 bell pepper
- 1 onion
- 1 ½ tbs pepper
- 2 cups chicken breast

DIRECTIONS

1. Heat ½ cup chicken broth.
2. Saute the onion, celery, garlic, carrot, and pepper for 5 minutes.
3. Add water and vegetable broth.
4. Stir in the lentils.
5. Cover and bring to a boil.
6. Simmer for 25 minutes.
7. Stir in the cumin, pepper, herbs, curry, and salt.
8. Simmer uncovered for 20 minutes.
9. Add the chicken during the last 5 minutes.
10. Stir in the lemon juice.

SHRIMP CHOWDER

Serves: **6**

Prep Time: **10** Minutes

Cook Time: **10** Minutes

Total Time: **20** Minutes

INGREDIENTS

- 3 tsp oil
- 4 sweet potatoes
- 1 cup spinach
- 1 tsp pepper
- 2 tsp salt
- 3 carrots
- 1 15-ounces coconut milk
- 3 cups almond milk
- 1 tsp curry paste
- 1 onion
- 1 tsp vanilla
- 1 lb shrimp
- 1 cup peas
- 8 celery stalks

DIRECTIONS

1. Sauté the potatoes, celery, carrots and onion in the oil for 5 minutes.
2. Add the coconut milk, almond milk, curry paste and vanilla.
3. Mix, then turn the heat down to a simmer.
4. Add the shrimp, spinach, peas and pepper and cook for 5 minutes.
5. Blend 1/3 of the soup, then pour the pureed mixture back to the pot.
6. Season with salt and serve hot.

DINNER

CHICKEN WITH CAULIFLOWER AND OLIVES

Serves: 4
Prep Time: 10 Minutes
Cook Time: 60 Minutes
Total Time: 70 Minutes

INGREDIENTS

- 1 bouquet thyme
- 1 head cauliflower
- ½ cup lemon juice
- 1 lb chicken breast
- 3 ½ tbs olive oil
- 1 ½ cup olives
- 4 cloves garlic
- 1 shallot
- 1 tsp salt
- 1 ½ tsp pepper
- ½ lemon zest

DIRECTIONS

1. Rinse the chicken breast and pat dry.
2. Spread the thyme springs in a baking dish.

3. Place the chicken over and add the cauliflower.
4. Mix the olive oil, olives, pepper, shallot, lemon juice and zest, garlic and salt.
5. Pour the mixture over the chicken.
6. Refrigerate overnight.
7. Bake at 400 for 1 hour.

ROSEMARY LEMON CHICKEN

Serves: **4**

Prep Time: **130** Minutes

Cook Time: **20** Minutes

Total Time: **150** Minutes

INGREDIENTS

- 3 cloves garlic
- ½ cup lemon juice
- 1 tsp salt
- 3 tbs oil
- 1 lb chicken breast
- ½ cup rosemary

DIRECTIONS

1. Mix the lemon juice, oil, rosemary, salt and garlic.
2. Rinse the chicken breast and pat dry.
3. Place the chicken breast in a baking dish.
4. Pour the mixture over and refrigerate for 2-3 hours.
5. Grill the chicken for 6 minutes on each side.

SALMON BURGERS

Serves: **12**

Prep Time: **10** Minutes

Cook Time: **30** Minutes

Total Time: **40** Minutes

INGREDIENTS

- 3 eggs
- 2 tbs flour
- ½ cup sesame seeds
- 4 tbs oil
- 2 tbs vinegar
- 2 cloves garlic
- 1 lb salmon
- 2 tsp ginger
- ½ cup scallions

DIRECTIONS

1. Rinse the salmon and pat dry.
2. Cut into cubes.
3. Mix the eggs, vinegar, scallions, 2 tbs oil, ginger, sesame seeds and ginger.
4. Add the salmon, then stir in the flour.
5. Form the mixture into patties.
6. Heat the rest of the oil in a frying pan.
7. Cook the patties for 5 minutes on each side.
8. Serve immediately.

ARGULA CUCUMBER SALAD

Serves: 2
Prep Time: 5 Minutes
Cook Time: 5 Minutes
Total Time: 10 Minutes

INGREDIENTS

- ½ tsp salt
- 4 cucumbers
- 3 tbs oil

- 6 ounces argula
- 2 tbs lemon juice

DIRECTIONS

1. Mix the ingredients in a large bowl.

TURKEY TACOS

Serves: 4

Prep Time: 10 Minutes

Cook Time: 30 Minutes

Total Time: 40 Minutes

INGREDIENTS

- 1 ½ cups tomato puree
- 1 ½ tbs lime juice
- 1 ½ tsp oil
- 1 lb turkey
- 1 avocado
- 1 onion
- 1 red pepper
- 3 tsp chile powder
- 1 ½ tsp oregano

- ½ tsp garlic
- 2 tsp garlic
- 2 tsp cumin

DIRECTIONS

1. Mash the avocado, then add the lime juice and garlic and mix.
2. Heat the oil in a pan, then add the red pepper and onions and saute.
3. Add ground turkey.
4. Add the cumin, oregano, garlic and chile powder.
5. Add the tomato puree after the turkey is well cooked and simmer for a little.
6. Fill the lettuce cups with the meat mixture and serve.

AVOCADO BACON AND EGGS

Serves: 2

Prep Time: 10 Minutes

Cook Time: 15 Minutes

Total Time: 25 Minutes

INGREDIENTS

- 2 eggs
- 2 tbs cheese
- 2 pieces bacon
- 1 avocado
- 1 tsp salt

DIRECTIONS

1. Preheat the oven to 425F.
2. Cut the avocado in half.
3. Scoop out some of the avocado.
4. Crack the egg inside the avocado.
5. Sprinkle some cheese and salt on top, then top with bacon.
6. Cook for 15 minutes.
7. Serve warm.

EGGS BAKED IN MUSHROOMS

Serves: 2

Prep Time: 10 Minutes

Cook Time: 20 Minutes

Total Time: 30 Minutes

INGREDIENTS

- 4 mushrooms
- 1 tsp black pepper
- 4 eggs
- 3 tbs cheese
- 3 tbs parsley
- 1 tsp garlic powder
- 2 tbs oil
- 1 tsp salt

DIRECTIONS

1. Preheat the broiler.
2. Line a baking sheet.
3. Season the mushrooms with the oil, ½ tsp salt, ½ tsp pepper and ½ tsp garlic powder.
4. Broil for 5 minutes on each side.
5. Remove from oven then set the temperature to 400.
6. Crack an egg into each mushroom.

7. Sprinkle some cheese on top, then bake for 15 minutes.
8. Sprinkle with the remaining seasonings and garnish with parsley, then serve.

TURMERIC CAULIFLOWER

Serves: 4

Prep Time: 10 Minutes

Cook Time: 20 Minutes

Total Time: 30 Minutes

INGREDIENTS

- 1 cauliflower
- 1 tsp black pepper
- 4 tbs oil
- 2 tsp turmeric
- 2 tsp salt
- 1 tsp garlic powder
- 2 tbs oregano

DIRECTIONS

1. Preheat the oven to 400F.
2. Chop the cauliflower.

3. Pour the oil over it.
4. Sprinkle the remaining ingredients over.
5. Bake for 20 minutes.

QUINOA SALAD

Serves: **4**

Prep Time: **10** Minutes

Cook Time: **20** Minutes

Total Time: **10** Minutes

INGREDIENTS

- 1 cup quinoa
- ½ cup cranberries
- 3 tsp olive oil
- ½ onion
- 1 bunch of kale
- 2 tsp salt
- 1 ½ tsp black pepper
- 1 cup feta
- ½ cup almonds
- 3 tsp lemon juice

DIRECTIONS

1. Cook the quinoa for 15 minutes in boiling salted water.
2. Drain in a sieve, then add the cranberries, cover and set aside.
3. Heat 1 ½ tsp oil and saute the onion.
4. Add the kale and cook for 5 minutes.
5. Season with salt.
6. Add the kale to quinoa, along with the feta and almonds and the lemon juice.

MEXICAN PIZZA

Serves: *4*

Prep Time: *10* Minutes

Cook Time: *20* Minutes

Total Time: *30* Minutes

INGREDIENTS
Pizza
- 1 ½ tsp cumin
- ½ tsp cayenne pepper
- 2 15-ounce cans black beans
- 8 corn tortillas
- 1 15-ounces can olives
- 3 tsp paprika
- 1 bell pepper

- 1 bunch green onions
- 1 cup cheese
- 1 red onion
- 4 tomatoes

DIRECTIONS

1. Preheat the oven to 400F.
2. Bake the tortillas until crispy.
3. Heat the black beans, cumin, paprika, and cayenne until smooth.
4. Divide the bean among the tortillas, then spread evenly.
5. Top with the onion, bell pepper, olives and tomatoes.
6. Sprinkle the cheese on top.
7. Bake for 10 minutes.

CHICKEN PIZZA

Serves: **4**

Prep Time: **10** Minutes

Cook Time: **20** Minutes

Total Time: **30** Minutes

INGREDIENTS

- 1 ½ tbs basil
- 1 cup pizza sauce
- 6 chicken strips
- 1 10-ounces garlic bread
- 1 ½ cup cheese

DIRECTIONS

1. Preheat the oven to 400F.
2. Place the garlic bread on a baking sheet.
3. Bake for 10 minutes, then spread the sauce over.
4. Cut the chicken strips and arrange over.
5. Sprinkle with cheese and basil.
6. Bake until the cheese melts.

TURKEY MEATLOAF

Serves: 4

Prep Time: 20 Minutes

Cook Time: 75 Minutes

Total Time: 95 Minutes

INGREDIENTS

- 1 egg

- 2 cups ketchup
- ½ cup bread crumbs
- 3 tbs soy sauce
- 2 ½ tsp basil
- 1 ½ tsp garlic powder
- ½ cup parsley
- 2 lb ground turkey
- ½ cup cheese
- 1 ½ tbs oregano
- 4 tbs Worcestershire sauce
- ½ cup oats

DIRECTIONS

1. Preheat the oven to 400F.
2. Mix together all of the ingredients until combined.
3. Form the mixture into a loaf shape.
4. Top with ketchup.
5. Bake for 75 minutes.

FRITTATA

Serves: **4**
Prep Time: **10** Minutes

Cook Time: *15* Minutes

Total Time: *25* Minutes

INGREDIENTS

- 1 cup spinach leaves
- 8 eggs
- 1 ½ tsp black pepper
- 1 red pepper
- ½ avocado
- 2 garlic cloves
- 3 tsp oil
- 3 tomatoes
- 1 ½ tbs thyme
- 1 ½ tbs marjoram
- 3 scallions
- 8 ounces chicken breast
- 2 tsp salt

DIRECTIONS

1. Preheat the oven to broil.
2. Heat the oil in a skillet.
3. Cook the scallions and the red peppers for 2 minutes.
4. Add the marjoram, tomatoes, garlic, thyme and chicken, salt and pepper.
5. Cook for a minute.
6. Add the spinach and cook for another minute.
7. Add the beaten eggs to the skillet and stir in a little until the eggs begin to set.

8. Put in the oven for 5 minutes, serve with avocado

SLOPPY JOE SLIDERS

Serves: **4**

Prep Time: **20** Minutes

Cook Time: **25** Minutes

Total Time: **45** Minutes

INGREDIENTS

- 1 ½ tsp vinegar
- 1 9-ounce can tomato sauce
- 8 hamburger buns
- 1 carrot
- 10 ounces ground beef
- 2 tsp garlic powder
- 1 ½ tsp chili powder
- ½ tsp black pepper
- ½ cup ketchup
- 1 tbs mustard
- 1 ½ tbs Worcestershire sauce
- 1 tbs tomato paste
- 1 cup onion

DIRECTIONS

1. Preheat the broiler.
2. Heat a skillet.
3. Great the carrot.
4. Cook the beef, carrot, and onion for 5 minutes.
5. Add the chili powder, garlic powder and pepper, then cook for another minute.
6. Mix the ketchup, mustard, Worcestershire sauce, vinegar, tomato pasta and tomato sauce.
7. Add the mixture to the skillet.
8. Simmer for 5 minutes.
9. Toast the halved buns.
10. Place the mixture on the bottom half of the bun, then cover with the top half.

SPINACH BALLS

Serves: *15*

Prep Time: *10* Minutes

Cook Time: *10* Minutes

Total Time: *20* Minutes

INGREDIENTS

- 1 ½ tbs butter

- 1 cup breadcrumbs
- 1 ½ tbs yogurt
- 2 tbs green onion
- 1 10-ounces package spinach
- 1 egg
- 1 tsp paprika
- 1 cup cheese

DIRECTIONS

1. **Mix all of the ingredients in a bowl.**
2. **Form balls.**
3. **Bake at 350F for 15-20 minutes.**

ZUCCHINI PIZZA

Serves: **6**

Prep Time: **25** Minutes

Cook Time: **15** Minutes

Total Time: **40** Minutes

INGREDIENTS

- 20 slices pepperoni
- 2 tsp herb seasoning

- 4 zucchini
- 1 ½ tsp salt
- 1 lb mozzarella

DIRECTIONS

1. Preheat the broiler.
2. Wash the zucchinis and cut off the ends.
3. Cut into even slices.
4. Spray a baking dish with non-stick spray.
5. Place the zucchini slices on the baking sheet.
6. Sprinkle with the salt and the herbs.
7. Cover with the grated cheese.
8. Broil until the cheese is starting to melt.
9. Place the pepperoni slices on top.
10. Broil for another 5 minutes, remove and serve

CARROT AND BROCCOLI NUGGETS

Serves: 4
Prep Time: 10   Minutes
Cook Time: 30   Minutes
Total Time: 40   Minutes

INGREDIENTS

- ½ tsp black pepper
- 1 ½ tbs oil
- 1 garlic clove
- 1 cup carrots
- 3 cups broccoli
- 2 eggs
- 1 ½ cup breadcrumbs
- 1 cup cheese
- ½ tsp onion powder

DIRECTIONS

1. Shred the carrots.
2. Steam the broccoli for 2 minutes.
3. Pulse together the carrots, garlic, onion powder, eggs, black pepper, 1 cup breadcrumbs for 10-15 seconds.
4. Form balls from the mixture.
5. Coat the balls with the remaining breadcrumbs.
6. Heat the oil in a skillet.
7. Cook the nuggets for about 5 minutes on each side.
8. Serve immediately.

PIZZA PASTA

Serves: *4*

Prep Time: *10* Minutes

Cook Time: *15* Minutes

Total Time: *25* Minutes

INGREDIENTS

- 2 cups cheese
- 2 cloves garlic
- 1 cup pepperoni
- 1 tsp oil
- 8 ounces sausage
- 2 cups tomato pasta
- 2 cups water
- 8 ounces rotini
- 1 onion
- 1 tsp salt
- 1 tsp black pepper

DIRECTIONS

1. Heat the oil in a skillet.
2. Add the onion and sausage and cook until the sausage is completely cooked.
3. Add the garlic and cook for another 30 seconds.

4. Add the pepperoni, pasta sauce and water and stir.
5. Stir in the rotini and bring to a boil.
6. Boil for 10 minutes.
7. Season with salt and pepper, then stir in the cheese.

CHICKEN VEGGIE BAKE

Serves: **4**

Prep Time: **25** Minutes

Cook Time: **35** Minutes

Total Time: **60** Minutes

INGREDIENTS

- 3 carrots
- 2 cups mushrooms
- 1 tsp thyme
- 1 ½ lb chicken breast
- 1 tsp salt
- ½ tsp black pepper
- 1 onion
- 1 cup cherry tomatoes
- 1 heat of broccoli
- ½ cup vinegar

- ½ cup oil
- 4 garlic cloves
- 4 tbs basil

DIRECTIONS

1. Preheat the oven to 400F.
2. Line a baking sheet with parchment paper.
3. Mix the oil, thyme, vinegar, pepper, salt, basil and garlic.
4. Place the chicken into 1/3 cup of the sauce.
5. Marinate for at least 15 minutes.
6. Chop the vegetables.
7. Place them on the sheet pan, except for the tomatoes.
8. Pour the rest of the sauce over, then add the chicken.
9. Bake for 10 minutes, then add the tomatoes.
10. Bake for another 10 minutes.
11. Top with basil.

CHICKEN WITH ROASTED PEPPERS

Serves: *4*

Prep Time: *10* Minutes

Cook Time: *30* Minutes

Total Time: *40* Minutes

INGREDIENTS

- ½ cup oil
- 1 cup chicken broth
- 2 tbs herbs
- 4 chicken breasts
- ½ cup vinegar
- 4 garlic cloves
- 1 onion
- 4 bell peppers
- 1 tbs basil

DIRECTIONS

1. Preheat the oven to 375F.
2. Place the onion and pepper slices in a bowl.
3. Mix the oil, vinegar, garlic, broth and herbs together.
4. Pour the mixture over the peppers and onion.
5. Place the chicken breasts in a baking pan.
6. Season with salt and pepper.
7. Pour the pepper and onion mixture on top.
8. Cover with foil and bake for 40 minutes.
9. Serve immediately.

DESSERT

PUMPKIN BISCUITS

Serves: *8*

Prep Time: *10* Minutes

Cook Time: *30* Minutes

Total Time: *40* Minutes

INGREDIENTS

- ½ cup pumpkin
- 1 tsp rosemary
- 1 tsp thyme
- ½ tsp salt
- 1 tsp baking powder
- ½ cup oil
- 1 cup flour
- 2 tbs milk
- 2 tbs honey
- 3 eggs

DIRECTIONS

1. **Preheat the oven to 350F.**

2. Mix the pumpkin, coconut milk, eggs, honey, oil, and herbs in a bowl.
3. In another bowl mix the flour, salt, and baking powder.
4. Mix the dry and the wet ingredients together.
5. Line a baking sheet with parchment paper.
6. Form balls from the dough and place onto the baking sheet.
7. Bake for 30 minutes.

SESAME ALMOND BARS

Serves: **16**

Prep Time: **10** Minutes

Cook Time: **25** Minutes

Total Time: **35** Minutes

INGREDIENTS

- 1 ½ cup sesame seeds
- ½ cup almonds
- ½ cup butter
- 2 ½ tbs honey
- 1 cup shredded coconut
- 1 tsp vanilla
- ½ tsp salt

DIRECTIONS

1. Preheat the oven to 350F.
2. Mix all of the ingredients.
3. Line a pan with parchment paper.
4. Push the seeds mixture evenly into the pan.
5. Bake for 25 minutes, remove and serve

STRAWBERRY CUPCAKES

Serves: **12**

Prep Time: **10** Minutes

Cook Time: **30** Minutes

Total Time: **40** Minutes

INGREDIENTS

- 3 eggs
- ½ cup milk
- 1 cup strawberries
- 2 tsp stevia
- 1 ½ cup flour
- 2 tsp baking powder
- 1 tsp salt
- ½ cup oil

- 2 tsp vanilla

DIRECTIONS

1. Preheat the oven to 350F.
2. Line a muffin tin with muffin papers.
3. Crack the eggs in a bowl.
4. Blend the strawberries and milk until smooth.
5. Add the vanilla, stevia, flour, salt and baking powder and whisk together.
6. Add the oil and whisk.
7. Divide into the muffin tin.
8. Bake for 35 minutes.

PIZZA SNACKS

Serves: **4**

Prep Time: **10** Minutes

Cook Time: **35** Minutes

Total Time: **45** Minutes

INGREDIENTS

- 1 jar marinara sauce
- ½ cup tomato paste

- ½ tsp oregano
- 2 tbs parsley
- ½ cup tomatoes
- ½ tomato sauce
- 3 tbs oil
- ½ cup onion
- 2 garlic cloves
- ½ tsp basil
- 2 tsp salt
- 2 zucchinis

DIRECTIONS

1. Heat the oil in a pot.
2. Saute the onion for 3 minutes
3. Add the garlic and saute for 2 more minutes.
4. Stir in the remaining ingredients.
5. Simmer for 30 minutes.
6. Preheat the oven to 400F.
7. Cut the zucchinis half length-wise.
8. Use the zucchinis as base and top with the sauce.
9. Add your desired toppings.
10. Bake for 20 minutes.
11. Allow to cool, then serve.

ROASTED CRISPS

Serves: **12**

Prep Time: **10** Minutes

Cook Time: **30** Minutes

Total Time: **40** Minutes

INGREDIENTS

- 6 tbs oil
- 5 cups jicama
- 4 cups sweet potatoes
- 4 cups red beets
- 2 tsp salt
- 3 drops blue food dye

DIRECTIONS

1. Line the sheet with parchment paper.
2. Preheat the oven to 375F.
3. Peel and slice the red beets.
4. Toss with 2 tbs of oil.
5. Spread on the baking sheet.
6. Roast for 10 minutes, then flip over.
7. Toss the peeled, sliced jicama with 2 tbs of oil.
8. Spread on the baking sheet, bake for 10 minutes, until edges turn golden.

9. Toss the peeled and sliced sweet potato with 2 tbs of oil and food dye.
10. Bake for 10 minutes.

POPSICLES

Serves: *8*

Prep Time: *10* Minutes

Cook Time: *30* Minutes

Total Time: *40* Minutes

INGREDIENTS

- 2 cups strawberries
- Stevia
- 2 cans coconut milk
- 2 drops food dye

DIRECTIONS

1. Blend the strawberries with 2 tbs of water and 3 drops of stevia.
2. Whisk 1 cup coconut milk with 3 drops of stevia.
3. Whisk the other cup with the food dye.
4. Freeze the strawberries for 20 minutes filling 1/3 of a popsicle mold.

5. Fill the other 1/3 with the stevia coconut milk, and the rest with the colored coconut milk.
6. Freeze at least 3 hours.

BUTTER CUPS

Serves: **12**

Prep Time: **10** Minutes

Cook Time: **0** Minutes

Total Time: **10** Minutes

INGREDIENTS

- 2 tbs oil
- 8 ounces chocolate
- 12 candy paper
- ½ cup almond butter

DIRECTIONS

1. Line a muffin pan with candy paper.
2. Heat 3 ounces of chocolate with some oil in the microwave for 30 seconds.
3. Cover the bottom of each muffin paper with the melted chocolate.
4. Put in the freezer for 5 minutes.

5. Melt the remaining chocolate.
6. Drop balls of nut butter in the middle of each cup.
7. Spoon the remaining chocolate into the cups.
8. Freeze for 15 minutes.

BEET & CAULIFLOWER TORTILLAS

Serves: *12*

Prep Time: *10* Minutes

Cook Time: *30* Minutes

Total Time: *40* Minutes

INGREDIENTS

- 6 eggs
- 1 heat cauliflower
- 1 red beet
- 2 ½ tbs oil
- 2 cups almond meal

DIRECTIONS

1. Preheat the oven to 375F.
2. Line 2 cookie sheets with parchment paper.

3. Cut the cauliflower and beets in chunks.
4. Chop, using a food processor.
5. Combine the cauliflower beet mixture with the almond meal and eggs in a bowl.
6. Create tortillas from the batter and place on the cookie sheet.
7. Bake for 8 minutes, then flip over and cook for another 5 minutes.

BLUEBERRY MUFFINS

Serves: **12**

Prep Time: **10** Minutes

Cook Time: **30** Minutes

Total Time: **40** Minutes

INGREDIENTS

- ½ cup almonds
- 1 tbs maple syrup
- 2 tbs coconut butter
- 8 eggs
- 2 tsp vanilla
- 3 tbs maple syrup
- 12 muffin papers

- 2/3 cup flour
- ½ cup erythritol
- ½ cup coconut milk
- ½ cup coconut butter
- 1 ½ cup blueberries
- 1 tsp salt
- 1 ½ tsp baking powder
- ½ tsp cinnamon
- ½ cup almond meal

DIRECTIONS

1. Preheat the oven to 350F.
2. Line the muffin tin pan with muffin papers.
3. Whisk the flour, salt, baking powder, and cinnamon.
4. Add the eggs, vanilla, maple syrup, erythritol, coconut milk and coconut butter.
5. Whisk well.
6. Fold in the blueberries.
7. Distribute the batter into the muffin cups.
8. Sprinkle the almonds on top.
9. Bake for 30 minutes, then serve warm.

CHOCOLATE THINS

Serves: **24**

Prep Time: **30** Minutes

Cook Time: **0** Minutes

Total Time: **30** Minutes

INGREDIENTS

- 2 tsp vanilla
- ½ cup cacao nibs
- 1 tsp salt
- 16 ounces chocolate
- ¼ cup oil
- 3 tsp peppermint oil

DIRECTIONS

1. Line a cookie baking sheet with parchment paper.
2. Melt the chocolate with the oil in the microwave for 1 minute.
3. Fold in the cacao nibs, salt, peppermint oil, and vanilla.
4. Pour the mixture on the parchment paper, creating a thin layer.
5. Place in the freezer for at least 20 minutes.
6. Cut into desired shapes.

DRINKS

ROOT BEER FLOAT

Serves: *1*

Prep Time: *5* Minutes

Cook Time: *0* Minutes

Total Time: *5* Minutes

INGREDIENTS

- 1 can root beer
- ½ cup vanilla ice cream

DIRECTIONS

1. Pour the contents of can into a glass.
2. Add the ice cream
3. Serve immediately.

CHERRY SMOOTHIE

Serves: **2**

Prep Time: **10** Minutes

Cook Time: **0** Minutes

Total Time: **10** Minutes

INGREDIENTS

- 1 dropper stevia
- 3 kale leaves
- ½ cup nuts
- 1 tbs chia seeds
- 1 cup cherries
- 8 ounces almond milk
- 1 cup spinach
- 1 scoop protein powder
- 1 tbs greens

DIRECTIONS

1. **Blend all of the ingredients together.**
2. **Serve cold.**

PUMPKIN CAPPUCCINO

Serves: 2

Prep Time: 10 Minutes

Cook Time: 0 Minutes

Total Time: 10 Minutes

INGREDIENTS

- 2 tsp cinnamon
- 10 drops stevia
- 2 tsp pumpkin pie spice
- 1 pot coffee
- 2 cups almond milk
- 1 tbs oil

DIRECTIONS

1. Brew a pot of coffee.
2. Heat 2 cups of almond milk.
3. Pour 2 cups coffee, warm milk and all of ingredients in the blender.
4. Blend for 20 seconds, then serve.

MORNING SMOOTHIE

Serves: 2

Prep Time: 5 Minutes

Cook Time: 0 Minutes

Total Time: 5 Minutes

INGREDIENTS

- ½ cup cranberries
- 2 cups spinach
- 1 chard leaf
- 2 scoops protein powder
- ½ cup cherries
- 20 ounces almond milk
- 2 droppers stevia
- 3 tbs coconut butter
- 4 leaves mint
- 1 handful of ice

DIRECTIONS

1. Blend all of the ingredients together.
2. Serve immediately.

MANGO PASSION SMOOTHIE

Serves: 2

Prep Time: 5 Minutes

Cook Time: 0 Minutes

Total Time: 5 Minutes

INGREDIENTS

- 2 scoops protein powder
- ½ cup spinach
- 2 kale leaves
- 1 handful of ice
- 2 packets stevia
- 8 ounces almond milk
- 1 mango
- 1 banana
- 8 ounces water
- 1 scoop greens
- 2 tbs flax seeds
- 2 tbs coconut butter

DIRECTIONS

1. Blend for 30 seconds.
2. Serve immediately.

HEARTBEET SMOOTHIE

Serves: 1
Prep Time: 5 Minutes
Cook Time: 0 Minutes
Total Time: 5 Minutes

INGREDIENTS

- 1 scoop protein powder
- 1 cup ice
- 1 cup red beet
- 1 tbs hemp seeds
- 1 cup almond milk
- 1 tbs cacao powder
- 2 tsp cinnamon

DIRECTIONS

1. Blend until smooth.
2. Serve.

ENERGY SMOOTHIE

Serves: 2

Prep Time: 10 Minutes

Cook Time: 0 Minutes

Total Time: 10 Minutes

INGREDIENTS

- 20 ounces iced green tea
- 1 cup ice
- 2 cups spinach
- 2 kale leaves
- ½ cup raspberries
- ½ cup blackberries
- 2 scoops protein powder
- 2 droppers stevia
- 2 tbs avocado

DIRECTIONS

1. Blend for 30 seconds.
2. Serve cold.

CHOCOLATE SMOOTHIE

Serves: 2

Prep Time: 5 Minutes

Cook Time: 0 Minutes

Total Time: 5 Minutes

INGREDIENTS

- ½ avocado
- 8 ounces almond milk
- 1 tbs cacao nibs
- 1 tbs greens
- 2 tbs cacao
- 1 dropper stevia
- ¼ cup almonds
- 2 tbs coconut
- 1 scoop protein powder
- 1 cup ice
- 1 banana

DIRECTIONS

1. **Blend until smooth.**
2. **Serve cold.**

START SMOOTHIE

Serves: 2

Prep Time: 5 Minutes

Cook Time: 0 Minutes

Total Time: 5 Minutes

INGREDIENTS

- 1 scoop protein powder
- 1 tbs greens
- 1 dropper stevia
- 2 cups spinach
- ½ cup blueberries
- ½ cup cherries
- 2 chard leaves
- 2 tbs hemp seeds
- 2 tbs butter
- 1 ½ tbs goji powder
- ½ banana
- 8 ounces coconut water

DIRECTIONS

1. Blend until desired consistency.
2. Serve cold.

ANTIOXIDANT SMOOTHIE

Serves: **2**

Prep Time: **10** Minutes

Cook Time: **0** Minutes

Total Time: **10** Minutes

INGREDIENTS

- 2 tbs chia seeds
- 2 tbs coconut butter
- 8 ounces water
- 1 cup ice
- 2 tbs pomegranate powder
- ½ cup pomegranate seeds
- 1 cup strawberries
- 2 scoops protein powder
- 2 droppers stevia
- 16 ounces iced tea
- ½ cup spinach
- 2 leaves kale
- 1 scoop greens

DIRECTIONS

1. **Blend for 30 seconds.**

2. Serve cold.

THANK YOUR FOR READING THIS BOOK!

Made in the USA
Monee, IL
30 November 2023